WATCH
GO HOME

(Diary of a Daughter)

By:

Mary Mole-Murray

WATCHING DAD GO HOME

Copyright © 2023

Mary Mole-Murray

All rights reserved.

INTRODUCTION
Watching Dad Go Home

This book is a recollection via the memory and volatile actions of a daughter's experiences when her father of 87 years dies. The author will let you in on her daily diary of this most trying yet educational and meaningful chapter of her life.

As Mary sees the need to take the helm of being the daughter that eventually moves in with her father as he adjusts to being without his wife of more than 50 years. She serves as his caretaker alongside Hospice to ensure that all of her father's needs and wishes are realized.

The book focuses on her upbringing and the close relationship and important part that a father plays in the lives of their children.

Her experiences of the pain and emptiness yet strength of her family values to carry on in such an event.

Mary is motivated by love, commitment, and servanthood to ensure that her father's life is filled with the joy of having his five children around to continue the laughter and joy; thus, helping fill the void in his life. She serves as the helping servant and company keeper of her father after her mother passes eleven years earlier.

This book will cause you to see the devotion of a father, through the eyes of a daughter. She shares the highlights of a father who was such a great provider for her and her siblings.

A father who gave examples of the Christlike behaviors; a comedian, a strong man and very proud World War II Veteran for the sake of his country and family.

Through poetry and sometimes sharing comical events in this family, this book will make one come close to realizing the inevitability of death; and encourage the reader that, this is a part of life that we all will or have faced at some time in our lives whether it be the loss of a close friend, a mentor or family member. The book is tainted with real time daily living, with a Christian undertone that would encourage one to believe that there is a higher power that will always be present before, during and after the loss of a special person in one's' life. Ensuring the reader that just as good memories are important; they are forever; The author endeavors to convince every reader that 'Life does go on' and we are in a better state as a result of our good experiences.

I have written a documentary of a daughter's experience while she serves in the capacity of caretaker of her father – while she is close by daily as he transitions. The tone of this book is inspirational, with some Christian emphasis.

She leaves her career as a mental Health Counselor to care for her dad and thought, "He would have done the same for me." She heard an inspirational speaker who spoke to her unspoken words, "I have to take care of Dad." She was enlightened as this orator says that she should instead say: "I GET TO TAKE CARE OF DAD". Wow that is really the ultimate truth. She often heard her mom's voice saying, "Lizzy take care of your Daddy"; so, she not only "gets" to take care of him, but also watch him go home.

This book will share some intimate experiences of watching someone who has inspired your entire being – transition from life as we know it into eternity. I trust you will read not with personal information gathering, but to see the beauty of and results of the love of a father – his life values –experienced by a daughter.

Table of Contents

WATCHING DAD GO HOME

GO HOME

(Diary of a Daughter)

5/30/13

It's 10 p.m. after giving meds to help Dad sleep as I eat my late supper and get ready for bed, it hits me... 'Dad's going home' – I feel the tear ducts swell but remembering all the responsibility and business of tomorrow, and maybe even tonight I'd better not have a pity party- I need the rest.

HOW DO I PRAY? First, I say in my heart "Thy will be done" but was it really from my heart? Praying in my heavenly language as I rub his head, I watch Dad's expressions change as he connects with God, he taught me to trust and ask for anything – tonight I ask for a restful night for Dad. "The nurses say it's restlessness" but when they all left the room, those strong hands that held me and held and rocked my three girls to sleep many nights as I studied; were *vividly,* clearly waving good bye – I try to still them by gently covering them with my hands – but he whispers to me as if its only for my ears or as if he's telling me a secret: "I'm finished", "It won't be long", "bye-bye". I try to divert him, and he just squeezes my hands and shows such contentment in his face.

Caring for dad daily for the past 10 years came naturally. It was always my priority. I was the chosen (to do this) one of 5 siblings. I hated to shave Dad – he was my Super Man I didn't want to invade his manhood but now it was time for me to be strong and do what he taught his children be Independent and productive; do what you have to do to make things right. (Dad could do this (shave) himself at age 87 and most times he insisted on doing it often up until his last two weeks of life. I often heard my mom's voice saying, "Lizzy take care of your Daddy"; so "I get to take care of him".

MY HERO
MY WARRIOR

Dad was not just a father but DADDY. Dad the provider:_My Dad was always a great provider. He worked on the Railroad laying the heavy cross ties (manually). My mom taught us to honor and be proud of him – thus we spent a lot of our play time singing songs like "I've been working on the railroad". I would sing it and think of Dad coming home at the end of a long day. I would run down the dirt road to meet him and take that metal lunch bucket out of his hand – he always ate ¾ of his sandwich and left the other ¼ for me and left just a little tea in the thermos.

For some reason, this job ended. I'm sure it was due to modern times and equipment inventions and improvement. My dad would often tell this story in church (repeatedly as he aged): "I was hunting one night I laid my gun down by a stump and knelt on the stump and said Lord I need a good job to take care of my family". Dad shares with the family later that he was led to go to the United Door Company in town for a job. Even though anyone hired had to be referred or recommended by an employee or staff, Dad said he had no one but God (to recommend him). He watched anxiously as the manager points out one man at a time from a large group; when he was about to walk away, he points at my Dad and say, "You come – when can you start; dad said 'today" and the rest is history. My dad worked over 25 years as this factory went through two name changes (owners). He said, "it was not all good days, but God gave me this job and I won't quit". Dad retired with benefits to be able to enjoy his life to age 87.

Daddy sold his hunting catches (raccoons & opossums) to friends and neighbors to provide for us. He and mom also got a business license and drove to many places including Florida to sell the Raccoon Hides (Coon Hides).

Dad was my hero for many reasons, but most of all because he was to me the strongest man I knew. I've seen dad tackle the wild from 12 ft alligators, popping long poisonous snakes in half, taming feisty raccoons, to going into a burning house to save a neighbor's refrigerator from a house fire, standing up to bullies to defend us, to holding a red-hot pipe in his hand to place it back on the wood heater to continue to have heat in the little church house. Last but not least, those same hands would chastise me with his belt; really letting me know his strength, then showering me with the genuine love of a father assuring me that it was done in love.

Is one's strength in his words? Is it in their muscles, physique, strong confident protective words, things they could do, or firm looks? if it were then what do we glean from or lean on when all of these external strengths are transferred to a deep whisper, frail bodies, short steps that use to be so fast and rushing; now trusting and depending on the one(s) that you've mentored and taught to be strong!!

Yes, strength is not in the visible, tangible things we see... we learn what it was that we really gained from... it's the life lived - the life examples that reinstates the strength and faith in God that we thought was material. *My hero, my warrior – is within*; and confirmed as he taught us true Christianity through belief in the word of God... "Trust in the Lord with all your heart and lean not to your own understanding- in all thy ways acknowledge him and he will direct your paths..." no weakness here- only strength. God is our refuge! In him (God) is no weakness at all.

My dad has been healthy all of his 87 years of life. On May 7, 2013, he was diagnosed with kidney failure (not even heredity). A man that routinely took care of his basic needs and enjoyed watching nature was suddenly slowed down to lying in his bed with no desire to thrive. His mood was always a pleasant one. His favorite sayings as he declared, "I have to accept the things I cannot change" and "we none can stay here always". These may be truth, but it is null and void when you've been such a great and close loved one all of your life. As dad slowed down for the next few weeks, my life was dedicated to being there for him as much as possible, at any cost.

MY DADDY!
(I call him Dad dee – He called me Lizzy)

A note from dad

FOR MY GOOD

6/7/2013

Daddy had a good night – as I toggle back and forth from the Ativan to the Ambien ... I choose to believe that we and our caring gestures can make things better and make things happen. Thus, I choose to attribute the good night rest to my special prayer and lullaby to him before the meds were even given. Prescribed as often as needed; well, none since 7pm and its about 9:30- he sleeps all night peacefully...the bed alarm goes off when he moves; ooh I forgot to turn it on and when I did around midnight it only beeped from his softly moving to reposition and continue his rest. Humm that word; REST – didn't my Pastor just pray for me over the phone around 6pm that I and dad would get some rest!

It's the next morning. As I tugged and pulled to get him dressed for the day... so many thoughts ride in and out of my mind; what a struggle for a small lady as myself to maneuver that supposedly weak body around; Now I knew why I had law enforcement training to be able to maneuver a large body from one place to safety. I had to be determined and focused on the outcome... moving this body to safety... and KISS... Yeah it was the law enforcement jargon "Keep It Simple Stupid!" (lol)

Yes, I kept it simple as my hands were hurting (from my own health challenges) and yes, the trained Home Health Aide would be here at 9am, yes, my daughter who is an RN can accomplish this in 5 minutes, but she was in bed – and the need was now (7 am) and love doesn't always wait. When I began to use my hurting hands to bathe and dress daddy, pain became unimportant, not even an issue –this is the way we need to be in life. When you are determined to accomplish, you can't focus on the struggle the resistance or the pain... *You must focus on the outcome.*

When mom left 11 years ago there was no greater feeling of helplessness than to hear dad for months tell everyone we came in contact with strangers; dentists, opticians, whoever it was, he would say "I lost my wife –she slipped off from me." The experience of not having someone that has been with you for 52 years. During this time, I did not allow myself to grieve openly for my mother, because of my daddy! He was my strength, he held onto me as if I may leave also.   He was my strength, and I was his. Even though dad held on to me tight for two years, he was always clear and verbal that each of his children was special and equal in his love for them.   It made me think of the song about mothers but change it to: "A father loves his children all the time".

I remember those bare feet patting on the floor as he played guitar for me to sing...they now look the same to me. They walked to fishponds for a good seafood meal–they walked through the woods to find pleasure in hunting–most of all they carried him to the railroad tracks, through the industrial door factories, and especially through the fox holes in Okinawa getting frost bitten feet so badly that he felt like he was walking on pieces of hard wood. All of this he did Just so his children could have a better life. Wow! How similar to Jesus who walked all over the earth doing his father's will even to the cross receiving the nails in his feet, why? Same deal – so that we could live a better life.

"**How beautiful are the feet of him that teach the gospel of peace...**"

–Romans 10:15 KJV

And the Lord, who also has a song in his voice, began to sing in my ear; 'for my good' for my good' things will work out for my good. I could hear it in my spirit until I was given utterance and ... I sang in my exhausted voice: even though I would change things if I could... Things will work out for my good.

MY SUPERMAN

My father always taught my brothers to be tough mentally and physically – he and my brother, his youngest son (Andrew), always greeted each other with a handshake (must be that Veteran stuff, lol) well as he always told his youngest son, and this was always repeated; their little clique words: "Much of a Man" now I'm watching him moving forward in this life and I can say first-hand "he's much of a man".

Sometimes I thought I was in a war for a few minutes that felt like an hour (lolololol). I thought I had control of him one way and he was in control two to three ways! Somebody tell me what is this? I know he knew judo... but he's unable to stand alone now. I saw those tactics – not violent just focused like a pit bull! or should I say it like he always reminded everyone "I'm a WWII VETT TRON!" Yes, he is!! As I tried to figure out why I was helpless and not making any progress in moving him in the bed, time to call my brother Andrew, Superman Jr. He was there in a jiffy and took care of the situation gently. I saw him cross his legs at the ankle and thought, 'you might as well quit'! Once I stopped trying to roll him over to see why I was not doing anything – his hand was gripped on the bed rail, and he was relaxing. I said "this man is surviving the enemy while lying on his back". Wow! Then he would every now and then when he succeeded raise that victory fist in the air. No, he was not combative; just letting me know that he was still in control not wanting to be bothered. It was altogether different if I was doing what he told me to do.

As I watched my superman's physical strength deteriorate; Even In his appearance of weakness, he was strong. For the strength of his hand and feet never left. I know, because he held my hands within his. As he always did!

MY PRAYER

JUNE 8, 2013

Well its' June 8, 2013; As I daily walk to dad's bed side for the past two weeks and comfort him with my presence, dad would always reach for my hand and held it tightly as to comfort me. I asked the question that I asked a week ago when he said "verbally" to me "bye bye" - I'm finished" and smiled at me. I asked dad are you ready to go? You tired? He nodded his head yes to me and I sang to him the song, Everything Will Be Alright. He reached for my hand held it more gently this time. I started our prayers; this time I talked to him about all the things I knew he loved and was concerned about his church, his children, his grands, and great grands.

"Daddy you taught us well! – you've given us everything we need to make it in life. Everything will be Alright- your grands are grown and guess what? 'That CJ we were all concerned about!   Well, all the visitors you had the other day and the crowds outside? We were celebrating CJ's graduation. Daddy said "yeaah?" And I said "yeah!! He's gonna be fine." I continued, "so daddy you can take your rest we're gonna be fine." I sang the Lord is my light and my salvation (mom's favorite). Dad calmly dosed off to sleep.

I went off to my room for the night to nap with my routine being that I got up every hour to check on him, however at 6 am even though it was less than an hour before I last checked; I felt and urge to hurry in case he wanted to get up to use the bathroom. Well, he was resting so peacefully breathing so softly – I didn't even fluff his pillow as I often did. I just went back to bed.

JUNE 9, 2013

It's now 7:30 am June 9th, time to check on him again. I walk up to his beside – he is so still but in a different way... I call to him 'Daa day' and again Da dee (my pet name I always call him as only he would call me Liz-zee) "he didn't respond – I reached to rub his chest and felt the coolness of his folded hands, the coolness of his strong cheeks – the voice within said "he's gone". I called to my daughter who is an RN (sleeping in the next room). She confirmed it. The watch is over....
Daddy's gone home.

Watching dad go home was a spontaneous, unplanned part of my life... I'm his last born, he was always at my beckoning call... how do you do this? **Truly it was a sovereign move of the higher being – it's like life; you think you have control to a certain extent until you learn that life happens and so does death. I could only just be there for the ride.** The ride was like my favorite ride at the fair. it seemed only a moment and ends too quickly. So, here's the ride some days were simply no thoughts to write...

Last songs I led for Dad: As the crowds gathered in the funeral parlor, it swelled with neighbors, friends, and family from what seemed like half of the county. As they quietly watched our family view his handsome, 'casket sharp' body! Daddy lie in state. They seemed to be quietly watching for our reactions; A small voice said to me; " away with the sadness and the stillness, Daddy would want you to sing! Liz-zee! My head was down with short glances at Daddy; then I suddenly belted out with the song! "I Still Have a Praise" by Milton Bigham & the

Georgia Mass Choir. My grand-nephew (Tradd) joined me in leading the song, and the crowd seem to swell with joy.

NOTES OF EXPRESSION

I Momma appreciate the love and care you give Granddad. It's the same way Poochie and Granddad are. Poochie will let me handle her, feed her etc but her heart's set on Granddad - when he pulls up she opens her mouth and starts trying to speak - I'm not kidding

And Granddad - no matter what I do and the care I try to give - he only speaks about Lizzy (just like he did w/ Lit). Be encouraged - you're his rock - his anchor. (The whole family owes you a tremendous gratitude or our daddy/granddaddy might have already been gone from this earth in grief.)

Your Momma knows and she is well pleased with you 3

Your latter days shall be your Greater days because Tricia Jerri me Patrick Coy + CJ are going to make you very happy

Note written by Sophia, (my eldest daughter)

32

05/16/09

DEACON HAZEL MOLE.
     YOU ARE MORE THAN A DEACON OR A COUSIN YOU A AREA
MAN SENT FROM GOD TO TEACH AND HELP US YOUNG PEOPLE.

WE LOVE YOU AND ALWAYS WILL . WORDS COULD NEVER
EXPLAIN THE PERSON YOU ARE.

LOVE ALWAYS
QUEEN.

Note from dad's family, Queen & Latosha ("Neasey")

Watchful eyes and great-granddaughter,
Trinity, who called him "Gran-Mole"

Hazel Marvin Mole was a man of integrity and honor. As the head of our family, he wore many hats (and wore them with excellence). Thinking about my great-grandfather brings back more fond memories and emotions than I can keep up with. For the sake of being intelligible, I will attempt to summarize my memories of "Granda Mole" in a few short stories highlighting the beginning, middle, and end of the time that we shared together while he was on this earth.

Tribute from Great Grandson

By the time that I was born into our family, Grandad was in his early sixties. Still, I did not perceive him to be an elderly man because he did not carry himself that way. He was attached to his wife, "Grandma Mole", so you really could not think of one without the other.

Grandad and Grandma Mole lived right next door, so, my earliest perception of them was that I had really fun neighbors rather than great-grandparents. Of course I knew their names were "Grandma" and "Granda"; but, what does that mean to a toddler? In my mind, Grandma and Grandad were simply another set of parents who just happened to live next door instead of inside my house; and, that is how they treated me (like a son). I followed Granda everywhere; trying to wear his hunting gear, eat his food, ride on his lap when he drove his truck or lawn mower, carry his heavy equipment when was not looking, and anything else that your typical son would do when they idolize their father. Grandad was a superhero.

Patrick on his great-grandad's lawn mower

During Grade School:
Grandad as a Retiree

When I entered grade school I realized that Grandad was a great-grandfather and not a father. That realization made him even cooler in my eyes. One of the best things about Grandad was that he was always on the move. I can only remember seeing Grandad sick three times in the 21 years that I knew him. From as early as 5 am until as late as midnight, grandad was always on the move. He was retired by the time I was retired by the time I knew him, but that did not stop him from working tirelessly every day.

When I entered the second grade, I was asked to write about what I wanted to be when I grew up. Mrs. Blakewood (my second grade teacher) found my response particularly interesting because as a career choice I had decided that I wanted to be retired like my great-grandfather. You see, grandad worked so hard that he made retirement look like a profession. During this lesson that we were learning, I went home and asked Granda what he did for a living and his response was that he was retired. I assumed that retirement was a career that entailed: doing maintenance and landscaping for everyone in the neighborhood, collecting cans throughout the community to keep the neighborhood clean, building, hunting, fishing, trapping, and tanning fur. Of course, my teacher explained that retirement is a noteworthy end goal but I would have to find a different career in the meantime.

Grandad's Final Days:
What He Remembered

In his final years, Grandad slowed down a bit. While he never lost his physical strength or his strong will, Grandad's memory began to fade. I am not sure if it was Alzheimer's or Dementia, but he possessed the typical symptoms that come along with these diseases: getting lost, getting days mixed up, reverting to childhood memories, and asking the same thing over and over. While this is typically a sad phase of life to experience or witness, this stage of Grandad's life stuck out to me for a specific reason. In a time where he was losing or misplacing all of his memories, I found it interesting that there were things that Grandad never forgot. I believe that these things defined his true character.

First, Grandad never forgot who he was. I was always told that Grandad was a rough and tough man in his younger years. By the time I was born into our family, Grandad was a born-again Christian. Besides being physically strong as an ox, Grandad was gentle-natured and pure-hearted. I have heard many cases of people reverting back to swearing, being mean, or depressed when they developed Alzheimer's or Dementia. Grandad never forgot that he was a servant of God. Until his final days he was a deacon in our church. He was always the first to enter the building (turning on the lights and A.C.) and the last to leave (turning off the lights, shooing members out, and locking doors). In his final years, the message of the bible had been so engrained in his heart that he would instinctively finish any quote, verse, or statement that our poor pastor attempted to refer to during his sermons. Still, he was not overly prideful. Realizing that salvation is a process (not a destination) he routinely studied the bible and worked on his faith daily.

Last, Grandad never forgot who his family. Living next door, I had the time-consuming honor of helping him recall all of the members on our family tree over and over; telling him where they were and what they were doing. Sometimes Grandad would remember people in our family that I did not know. Sadly, that would usually indicate that the individual had passed. As Grandad reflected on the many people that had passed away over the years he would hold his head down solemnly in remembrance and ask God to "help him to accept the things that he could not change".

In his final days, Grandad's memory of specific family members diminished significantly. I decided to test him out one day by calling out names to him and the final response that he gave me is one that I will never forget. After playing the name game for a while, I looked at Grandad with a devilish smile and said, "Grandad you do not have a clue who I am, do you?" Grandad looked at me with twinkling eyes and gave me the same devilish grin. His response was, "I know that you're mine!" While names faded from his memory, everyone in the family occasionally ran through his mind. The example that he set for our family is etched into our hearts and minds; manifested in the way that we raise up every generation. Everyone in this family should remember that, "we are his children" and be proud of that fact.

–Note from Dr. Charles "Patrick" Magwood,
my grandson, dad's great grandson

6/10/13

My first night without dad – I'm tipping around not to disturb his rest. I'm in a semi daze, but I really think its denial??? Not ready to think about what just happened; so, I keep busy and depend on the Ambien at night to take me to the next morning. It's June 12th and the reality sets in that I really am relaxing, taking and enjoying a shower after many months of just going through the procedure. My thoughts are rambling as I get used to being in the house alone; I remember in April of 2002 when dad and I went to Florence, SC to get his new partials put in – he was sooo lost without mom. Everyone that came near, he would say to them "I lost my wife – she slipped away from me" I felt so helpless to help him.... Now it's 10 days after dad slept away from my presence and 'the cup has turned'. I go to the post office, I go to the variety store, and I start smiling and sharing with people I hardly know in the checkout line that my dad is gone.

6/16/2013

June 16th, my brain is in selective memory mode... so I don't even think about today is mom's birthday; she would have been 88. It's Sunday and the celebration is Father's Day. Midafternoon, I go to dad's grave to check on the florals and think of my great daddy – and wow I end up singing 'happy birthday to you' in honor of mom. Then my inner being spoke clearly... you can leave now **"this year it's Father's Day in heaven for him".** I had no tears, just that gentle smile he gave me covered my face as I moved on to my car.

6/21/2013

Today at 9:30 suddenly as the many many thank you cards are done – I "feel this fullness in my chest and face: Dad's gone home and I miss him!!"

7/2/13

Today I am so fixated and determined of the fact that it was not long after our moments of prayer and conversation that dad slept away and went home. I received the death certificate and complained to my daughter that the coroner's listed TOD (time of death) was not right; "they listed 7:15 am." My daughter texted me:

"Momma don't worry about it – Grand Daddy's in heaven now" So if I've watched him go home – I need not sweat the small stuff. Daddy's at home... And I was privileged to WATCH DAD GO HOME.

Lessons Learned

You never have to be there for your loved ones, you 'get to' be there

Instill good things in your peers and/or children; they will be there for a lifetime.

And the Lord who also has a song in his voice began to sing in my ear; 'for my good' for my good' things will work out for my good.   I could hear it in my spirit until I was given utterance and ... I sang in my exhausted voice: Even Though I Would Change Things If I Could... Things Will Work Out For My Good.

A GENTLE BREEZE

(At the gravesite)

Well, there's quietness again as they lower his coffin next to mom, Again I reminded the family of our legacy and again I led the family and crowd in singing one of Daddy's favorite songs:

"I'm Building a Home"

Lastly, The Military played: "Taps," all of the many florals were beautifully arranged around the gravesite:

Here comes this strong yet gentle breeze! It blew over the grave (just as it did at mom's burial 2/12/2002) My siblings, my daughters, and I just sporadically looked at each other in awe and amazement, SMILING. Because we all knew:

Dad's gone home and just got his wings!!!

Yes, Dad's gone home so here are a few after thoughts to close this chapter of my life.

DADDY, YOU'RE SUPER MAN!

(A reading to my Daddy)

I'VE HEARD OF THE SUPER MAN CLICHÉ' – BUT GUESS WHAT, YOU'RE TRULY A SUPERMAN.

THIS IS A LIST OF A FEW OF THE MILLION WAYS THAT I KNOW THAT BEHIND THAT CAPE YOU WEAR – THAT QUIET SMILE YOU'R REALLY SUPER MAN!

I don't remember my infant years, but Super Woman told me about it – how you took care of us while she was away – not only as the bread winner, but you could plait our hair.

*You braided my sister Vern's hair and took care of us

* I would see you returning from a hard day's work at the door factory- your legs seemed heavier for you to move than usual. I would run up the dirt road to meet you, because I knew that black lunch bucket that looks like a school bus had something good in it for me. Whatever you had for lunch you would leave me a piece of bread or a little piece of meat on the bone to tear the wax paper off and eat.

*When you got your bonus pay from work, I don't know how you got in those heavy silver dollars in your pocket, but you stepped in the door and beckoned all of us children to come and fill our little hand from your pocket ... you felt like a rich man; and to us, you were.

TABLES MADE OF DOORS: You knew how important it was for all of us to eat at the table together, so you made us a long table from the wood chips you brought home from the door factory – it was beautiful! Especially after super woman made and put a nice tablecloth on it.

WE WANTED A BATHROOM: You were the #1 outdoor toilet builder in the community; you built one for everyone who wanted one. You started building our bathroom little by little as the money was available. Our bathroom ended up being an empty room, but we still called it the bathroom and the place where we kept our portable bathroom stuff (smiling at Daddy).

CHURCH BENCHES MADE OF DOORS: Oh, what a scary day when you were building benches (pews) for our church; using the power saw the boss allowed you to use at work – you came in that day not with your lunch bucket, but your pants leg was torn and full of blood- you had an accident with the power saw; but guess what? You got stitches and superwoman helped you get better.

MUSIC IN THE HOUSE: There was always music in the house because you made the music playing your guitar. We would often see you sitting and reading the Bible, until you fell asleep. I would see you pick up the Bible to read and ask; Daddy are you getting ready to take a nap? You would strike up a tune and beckon me to come and guess the name of the song you were playing, then sing along while you played.

SPLINTER IN YOUR FOOT: You taught us that you were the King of the house and we treated you that way sometimes pampering your feet was and still is your favorite – I remember you called my sister, "Ann! Come get this splinter out of my toe" – Ann made a face that said: 'oh Lord here he goes' She said, "I'll make this one short". As he sat with his eyes closed ready to relax as she was trained to rub his toe softly to find the splinter. Ole Ann got a match, struck It (lit it), and stuck it to your toe… your eyes flew open as you jerked; Ann said: 'well if it was a splinter Daddy, I was going to light it". WE ALL HAD A GOOD LAUGH!

Lastly Daddy you taught us to show unconditional love and share with each other. I remember my new baby sister joining our family … you bought an orange can of baby powder with elephants on it … then you and mom said, 'this is for you to use for your baby sister'. That was so special.

MY SPIRITUAL DAD

Deacon Mole, with the Healing Hands:

Daddy was well known in the community and Lowcountry as 'Deacon Mole'. The one man who would lay his hands on you; pray and you would get instant results of healing. One of my treasures is passing the pond in Beaufort County South Carolina where my Daddy baptized me. I was so afraid of water, but as I walked toward the two Elders standing and waiting for me in the dark pond, I saw my Daddy standing there waiting also. Right then I knew I would be alright.

Spiritual Strength After A Great Loss

After the death of my mother, Daddy shared with family and the world the strength in his famous prayer: The Serenity Prayer. When asked how are you Mr. Mole? His response would be as would repeat daily and to family and others: With a smile he would say: "Accept the things I cannot change."

Daddy's Spirit Filled Gift of The Strings

Daddy's gift of music was so touching to all who came in contact with him. Though he could play the piano and organ, his favorite was the guitar. Daddy played and the people rejoiced and danced.

He also shared this gift with those wanting to learn to play. Many known guitarists in the Lowcountry were taught by daddy; To name a few were Deacon Frazier, of Yemassee SC, Pastor Jadon Buckner, of Walterboro, SC and the late Pastor Barry Mitchell of Columbia, SC.

He certainly influenced his grandson, Timothy Mole Sr., (Professional Musician and Producer) of Charlotte, NC.

Three of Dad's most favorite songs were: I Don't Know Why Jesus Loves Me, Go Down Jonah Go Down, and Beulah Land.

Daddy's Deep Spirit of Love of Country

Lastly, Daddy's instructions to me were: "[When I die], don't talk about my hunting hobby, or my fishing, then he smiled and said: "Let them know that I was a US World War II VET-TRAN" (veteran).

POEMS:

Bare Feet Patting on the Floor

"Lizzy – come here Lizzy!"

Daddy called with a great big smile

Didn't he know I was only 9?

The cheerful tunes from his guitar strings

"Name that song Lizzy" he would say-

As I watch those **bare feet patting on the floor**

The wide smile I gave made him play the more

Then I would just begin to sing

Oh, how it made him smile

That we enjoyed that gospel sound

As often at the end; I'd ease out like a train

Only to hear that call to do it all over again!!

Much of a Man My Superman!

Mom told me how you fought in your youth

But only if someone else was mistreated would you give em the boot

What a great fit for WWII

You fought for your country –still given em the boot

Very proud Technician 5

Wow how I wish you were still alive

You're much of a man my super Man

I knew I was right when I heard momma say to you:

You Da Man!"

And I'm thinking "that's MY Super Man!"

Its 10 pm and all are in bed

What's that sound pounding in my ear?

There's a horn blowing at my door

Maybe 3-4 racoons on his truck floor?

No its not! To my surprise

A 12 ft alligator rolled up by his side

He brought it to my house to get a picture

Lord have mercy daddy! The police gonna gitcha!

<u>LOVE IS</u>

A 1/2 stick of gum to share with your girls

The edge of the bread left for me

In your lunch box

Giving me a dollar when I was 20

And telling my mom: hush Liddie!

Rocking my babies/while I was at college

Making me go to church 3 times a week

To obtain real knowledge

When you said you were finished

I somehow knew that God was in it

You taught us well

I wish you could see

How we've excelled

So now take your rest

Because were truly the best!

TABLES MADE OF WOOD CHIPS

It was so important for family to eat together

Dad and mom -accomplished this whatever

How excited we were to see the finish product

Of this long 12 ft table

My Daddy was able

He glued together leftover chips from his job

Varnished it well while mom sewed a tablecloth

Oh the days we did enjoy

Our family gathered wisdom to be employed

Gatherings filling our hearts with joy

At this great table made of wood chips that's all.

ACKNOWLEDGEMENTS

My Support: Thelma B. Smith, Johnnie Mae Lester, Shirley White

Because you loved him: Richard & Irene Glover, the late Willie James Grant, Evangelist Elise Mcquire, Retha Mae McQuire, Bishop Herbert Alston, the late Deacon Melvin & Mary Jenkins, & the late Deacon James Patterson, Sr.

My Pastor: Christian Simmons

My siblings: Andrew, Hazel, Ann, Angie, Annette & Emmazine

My loving & spiritual coverings: Apostle Allen H. & Judge Janice Y. Simmons

My effectual prayer giant/first responder: *Bishop Paul S. Morton*

Right Hand Neighbors: *Willie & Ida Williams & family*

Watchful Eyes*: Regina Bowers-Robinson*

I am Grateful and Thankful!!

Amedysis Hospice Chaplain & Staff

To all of my close & surrounding counties that made me know that Dad was special

Vera Mae Campbell, Bessie Mae Grimes, Sally Ann Allen, Annette Kelly

Last but not the least:

My dearest daughters: Sophia, Patricia, and Jerolyn who supported me tremendously! through this journey.

Pictures top left: Daddy & his dog, Blue top right: Daddy & his boys middle left: Ann, Mom, Dad & Rambo (dog) bottom right: Daddy holding Travis (grandson) and Angie

Daddy &
granddaughter,
Kay

Daddy and
great-grandson,
Arden

Patricia, Daddy & Jerolyn
(granddaughters)

Daddy &
granddaughter, Patricia

Family Photo 1980 (Dad, Mom, children and grandchildren)

ABOUT THE AUTHOR

 Mary Murray (AKA Evangelist Mary Mole Murray, MDiv) is a graduate of the University of South Carolina and Tabernacle Bible College. She is an ordained Minister, and visionary. She is a retired certified Rehabilitative Mental Health Counselor, and Case Manager Counselor in the state of S.C. Department of Corrections who now operates in her God-given gifts of Evangelism and Visionary. She shares these insights and experiences through women's conferences,

which she established in the SC. Lowcountry in 2002. Her travels include revivals, prison Ministry and community-based outreach events. Mary is endowed with wisdom and anointing as a result of a life devoted to God, as displayed in this journal–like work designed to inspire, bless and motivate society via life lessons.

Did you enjoy this book? We would love to hear from you!

Mary Mole-Murray

marymurray71@gmail.com

www.deeperlifepress.com

Made in United States
Orlando, FL
22 March 2023